The Sponsor

The Dubois Branch of the Bank of Jackson Hole

is proud to be
the sole sponsor of this publication
for the benefit of the

National Bighorn Sheep Interpretive Center
at Dubois, Wyoming.

The directors and staff of the Bank of Jackson Hole trust you will find this authoritative book on the Rocky Mountain Bighorn Sheep both informative and enjoyable. Dubois, Wyoming, is privileged to be the home to the largest wintering Rocky Mountain Bighorn Sheep herd in North America. The Bank of Jackson Hole recognizes the valuable role that the National Bighorn Sheep Interpretive Center plays in the conservation of these majestic animals. Your purchase of this book helps insure the heritage of the bighorn sheep.

While in Dubois, be sure to visit the National Bighorn Sheep Interpretive Center and take a guided tour of the Whiskey Mountain Bighorn Sheep winter range. We invite you to also visit us at www.bighorn.org and www.bankofjacksonhole.com.

Tom D. Reed
Dubois Branch President
Bank of Jackson Hole
(Member FDIC)

BANK OF JACKSON HOLE
DUBOIS BRANCH

Rocky Mountain Bighorn Sheep

by
Dale E. Toweill

for the
**National Bighorn Sheep
Interpretive Center**
Dubois, Wyoming

Dedication

To my wife, Deyanne,
and to all those who love wild sheep
and wild places.

Copyright © 2007 by Dale E. Toweill

All rights reserved, including the right to reproduce this work in any form whatsoever without permission in writing from the publisher, except for brief passages in connection with a review. For information, please write:

The Donning Company Publishers
184 Business Park Drive, Suite 206
Virginia Beach, VA 23462

Steve Mull, General Manager
Barbara B. Buchanan, Office Manager
Richard A. Horwege, Senior Editor
Mellanie Denny, Graphic Designer
Derek Eley, Imaging Artist
Debby Dowell, Project Research Coordinator
Scott Rule, Director of Marketing
Tonya Hannink, Marketing Coordinator

Carey Southwell, Project Director

Library of Congress Cataloging-in-Publication Data

Toweill, Dale E.
    Rocky Mountain bighorn sheep / by Dale E. Toweill for the National Bighorn Sheep Interpretive Center.
      p. cm.
    Includes bibliographical references and index.
    ISBN 978-1-57864-410-0 (soft cover : alk. paper)
1. Bighorn sheep. I. National Bighorn Sheep Interpretive Center (Wyo.) II. Title.
    QL737.U53T694 2007
    599.649'7—dc22
                                        2007000311

Printed in the United States of America at Walsworth Publishing Company

Contents

Foreword 7
*by Suzan Moulton
& June Sampson*

Preface 9

Chapter 1:
Meet the Bighorn 10

Chapter 2:
Ice Age Relict 16

Chapter 3:
The Life of Bighorns 22

Chapter 4:
Communication
and the Rut 34

Chapter 5:
Bighorn Sheep
Management 44

Chapter 6:
Where to Watch
Bighorn Sheep 58

Index 62

**Suggested
Reading** 63

**Author's
Biography** 64

Foreword

You are about to begin a wildlife adventure: the discovery of Rocky Mountain bighorn sheep. You will be taking this adventure with one of best guides you can find, Dale Toweill. He is not only knowledgeable but enthusiastic. Soon you will be catching his excitement as he leads you into the high, rugged world of the bighorn. We hope that you will catch his "wild sheep fever" and travel to the high country to see the bighorns in all their majesty in person.

A visit to the National Bighorn Sheep Interpretive Center is also a great way to explore the world of the Rocky Mountain bighorn sheep—and less strenuous too! Here you can see dioramas of the rams clashing and the ewes with their lambs in the spring. Re-creations of the traps the Sheep Eater Indians used, exhibits that allow you to hear and even feel the bighorns, films, and high-tech interactive exhibits are all part of your experience at the Center.

During the winter months when the bighorns are on the wind-swept slopes of Torrey Rim or in the protection of Torrey Valley, the staff of the Center can take you out on a guided tour to see the Rocky Mountain bighorns. It is best to call ahead to make your reservation for this up-close-and-personal experience. School groups may also arrange for tours of the Center with special activities to help students to get the most from their visit. If your school is too far from the Center for a visit, you may borrow a trunk full of classroom resources and we will ship it to your school at a minimal cost.

This book plus the exhibits, guided tours, and school programs are all part of the educational efforts of the National Bighorn Sheep Interpretive Center. These educational programs are critical for the preservation of Rocky Mountain bighorn sheep in the twenty-first century. As hunter numbers dwindle and we become a more urban population, only an informed and concerned new generation will be capable of taking over the reins and safeguarding the bighorns. Thus ensuring future generations will be able to experience wild sheep, free to roam their historic ranges.

—*Suzan Moulton, Executive Director*
—*June Sampson, Former Executive Director*
National Bighorn Sheep Interpretive Center
Dubois, Wyoming

Preface

The Rocky Mountain bighorn sheep is a fascinating wild animal, the product of millions of years of adaptation to some of earth's most spectacular mountain habitats. I consider myself privileged to have studied and managed wild sheep. I never cease to marvel at the intimate relation of body form, behavior, and environment of these animals, and I hope that this small book will help you share my own sense of wonder and enjoyment as you consider these fascinating animals.

This book is the product of collaboration by many people. It would never have been written without the encouragement of June Sampson, former executive director of the National Bighorn Sheep Interpretive Center in Dubois, Wyoming and Carey Southwell, project director at the Donning Company Publishers. My good friend and life-long mentor, Dr. Valerius Geist, offered insights on bighorn sheep behavior. Photographs were provided by many people, but I am especially indebted to Tim Bernard for allowing me to use many of his outstanding pictures of bighorn sheep. My wife, Deyanne, not only encouraged me throughout preparation of this book but also all the years of effort and research that preceded and made it possible. Words cannot express my debt.

Chapter 1

Meet the Bighorn

Scotsman Duncan McGillivray killed the first Rocky Mountain bighorn sheep known to science on November 29, 1800. Several bighorn sheep were killed that day along Alberta's Bow River. The skins and skeletons were preserved and sent to England, where Dr. George Shaw described them in 1803, naming the species *Ovis canadensis*—"Canadian sheep."

"The buck that was killed might weigh about 190 or 200 pounds," Shaw wrote. He added in amazement: "thirty of which may be the weight of his enormous horns, which measured along the curve were 3½ feet long and 15 inches in circumference."

The name *Rocky Mountain bighorn sheep* evokes range and habitat, description and relationship. Animals of the Rocky Mountains, bighorns range from the Peace River of British Columbia south to northern New Mexico, and from the badlands of the Great Plains west across the Rockies to the Cascade Mountains of Washington and Oregon. Rocky Mountain bighorns occupy some of the most rugged terrain in this vast region.

Bighorn refers to the massive, curling horns of the males, and *sheep* is definitive—these are member of the scientific family of all sheep *(Ovis)*, a group that which evolved in central Asia and spread westward, arriving in North America across the Bering land bridge at least two hundred thousand years ago.

> "The buck that was killed might weigh about 190 or 200 pounds," Shaw wrote. He added in amazement: "thirty of which may be the weight of his enormous horns, which measured along the curve were 3½ feet long and 15 inches in circumference."

When McGillivray shot that first ram, the opening of interior North America was just beginning. Alexander Mackenzie had first crossed North America in 1793, one year after Robert Grey discovered the mouth of the Columbia River. When Thomas Jefferson became the third president of the United States in 1801, he longed to know what lay west of the Mississippi River—and as president he set a plan in motion for a great voyage of discovery.

Mature Rocky Mountain bighorn sheep, with their massive horns, sleek and compact bodies, and scars from earlier battles, seem to radiate raw power. (Photo by Dale Toweill)

The same year that Shaw published that first description of bighorns, Meriwether Lewis and William Clark were preparing to explore the area from the headwaters of the Missouri to the mouth of the Columbia River. No one knew what discoveries awaited. Jefferson speculated that Ice Age giants such as the mammoth and the ground sloth still wandered the land. Although his Corps of Discovery failed to locate these giants, they found bighorn sheep and other species that had evolved with them during the Ice Ages.

Bighorn sheep appear regal, with compact masses of muscle on a stout frame, brown coat trimmed in white, and massive curling horns. (Photo by Tim Bernard)

When the Corps of Discovery returned in 1806, their discoveries sparked intense interest. Bighorn sheep came to symbolize Western mountains, just as buffalo symbolized the Great Plains.

Bighorn rams are regal in appearance. Their bodies are compact masses of muscle on a stout frame, their coat chocolate brown trimmed with white on the muzzle, rump, belly, and legs. Rams may weigh over 350 pounds (most weigh 160 to 250 pounds) and stand thirty-eight to forty inches at the shoulder. Their golden wide-set eyes are situated well forward on the head, providing a wide arc of phenomenal vision. Their sense of smell is excellent and although their ears are small their hearing is acute.

The most striking feature of rams is the great, curling horns. Thin and sickle-shaped while rams are young, the horns grow in circumference and length, becoming nearly

The world's record bighorn sheep was killed by a hunter, Guinn Crousen, at Luscar Mountain, Alberta, in 2000. (Photo courtesy of Boone and Crockett Club)

Meet the Bighorn

Although bighorn sheep are nearly always brown with a white trim, there is considerable variation from very light to dark. The most unusual color is nearly all white, shown here. This is not an albino sheep; note the yellowish eyes and patches of brown hair. (Photo by Mike Foster)

circular at the base as the horn core thickens with age. Bases may reach sixteen to eighteen inches in circumference, and horn length forty to fifty inches by ten years of age. Rams may grow the largest horns of all ruminant (grazing) animals, that weigh more than forty pounds (8 to 12 percent of the animal's entire body weight)! Horns of the world record Rocky Mountain bighorn, killed in Alberta in 2000, were nearly four feet long with sixteen-inch bases.

Ewes also have horns. In fact, horns (or rather, tiny keratin-covered buds from which horns quickly grow) are evident even on newly born lambs. Horns grow quickly, reaching several inches in length during the lamb's first summer of life. However, in contrast with the massive horns of rams, the horns of ewes reach their maximum basal circumference and most of their eight- to nine-inch length by age three. Horns of young rams are as large as those of ewes by twelve to sixteen months of age, and by twenty-four to thirty months horn bases begin to expand, allowing young rams to be easily identified.

As the horns of rams continue to grow they begin to intrude on the ram's peripheral vision. At this point (by age five or six) rams begin to "broom" their horns, rubbing or breaking the horn tips. Most adult rams "broom off" the first two years of growth, the "lamb tips" that grow before bases begin to expand.

Even newborn lambs have horn buds that grow quickly. (Photo by Tim Bernard)

Bighorn sheep horns grow over a body core attached to the skull. Note the darker rings (or annuli) that mark the period when no horn growth occurs during the winter, which can be used to determine the age of bighorns. (Photo by Dale Toweill)

Horns are composed of keratin—the same type of hard material as human fingernails. Derived from skin cells, horn growth is related to diet and stress. Horn growth stops completely for a brief period each winter, creating clearly evident corrugations (annuli) on the horns. Biologists can determine a sheep's age by counting the annuli, and adjusting for brooming.

Ewes are smaller than rams, standing thirty-three to thirty-four inches at the shoulder and weighing 120 to 200 pounds. Lacking the huge horns and massive musculature of rams, ewes appear almost dainty. Appearances are deceiving, however—ewes negotiate steep cliffs and seemingly impossible rock faces with ease. Moving like a confident ballerina among the tiniest of ledges, ewes seem to ignore the consequences of a slip or tumble that could result in immediate death.

Female bighorn sheep, or ewes, also have horns, but they rarely grow longer than eight or nine inches. (Photo by Tim Bernard)

Meet the Bighorn

The image is of a ballerina among the cliffs is doubly appropriate, because like a ballerina bighorns walk on the tips of two toes. Their outer hooves are modified toenails, exquisitely shaped to grip any slight protrusion, while the base of the foot—the end of the toe—forms a soft pad that conforms to each surface preventing slippage. The cone-shaped foot is tightly wrapped with tendons, transferring the pressure from the hoof to the muscular legs—a marvel of engineering.

With their specially adapted hooves, bighorn sheep move with ease even among steep rocks. (Photo by Vic Coggins)

Chapter 2

Ice Age Relict

Jefferson's Corps of Discovery may have found no mammoths, but bighorn sheep were no less an artifact of the great Ice Ages. Ancestors of bighorn sheep evolved in Asia about 45 million years ago. These ancestral sheep grazed the abundant grasses of high central Asian plateaus that were forced ever higher as India's tectonic plate collided with Asia, a vast slow-motion collision that raised the Himalaya Mountains. Throughout the Quaternary Period (from 350,000 to as recent as 20,000 years ago) great Ice Ages—cycles of twenty or more great advances of glacial ice across huge expanses of North American and Asia, followed by interludes of relative warming and glacial retreat, reshaped the northern landscape. As sheets of ice formed and retreated, they pulverized rock, creating rich new soil that exploded with grasses each time glaciers retreated. Following the pulse of rich grazing, ancestral wild sheep gradually moved east across China and north into Siberia. Sheep crossed into North America across a vast plain of wet meadows and shallow lakes where the Bering Sea exists today, the product of sea level decline as ice built up on the land. The Bering "land bridge" formed many times, allowing animals to move both east and west. Warm interglacial periods allowed the newcomers to move south, and subsequent periods of glacial advance forced many to move even further south.

> "Sheep crossed into North America across a vast plain of wet meadows and shallow lakes where the Bering Sea exists today."

Bighorn sheep evolved to take advantage of the rich forage associated with retreating glaciers. (Photo by Tim Bernard)

As they moved into North America, wild sheep left wild goats, which also evolved in Asia but which failed to cross the Bering plains. Only two species of mountain goat (one extinct) were native to North America, and these two species were very specialized for life among the steepest mountain cliffs. No animals were adapted to exploit the rocky, rough mountains of North America—until wild sheep arrived. The fossil record from Natural Trap Cave in north-central Wyoming reveals a cold dry climate much like the plains of arctic Alaska today in this area twenty thousand years ago. Tall grasses flourished, producing abundant food for a wide variety of grazing animals—mammoths, muskoxen, camels, bison, pronghorns, and wild horses shared the plains and foothills with bighorns.

Predators were abundant as well. Siberian tigers occupied the Bering plains, and the American lion (25 percent larger than the largest living cat, the tiger) ranged as far south as Mexico. Two species of saber-toothed cats, an American cheetah, mountain lions, lynx, and bobcats also flourished, as did coyotes, timber wolves and their close

Mountain goats, with their all-white coats and short dagger-like horns, occupy many bighorn sheep ranges. (Photo courtesy Idaho Department of Fish and Game)

Mountain lions are just one among the many predators that evolved with bighorn sheep. Others include the now-extinct American lion, American cheetah, and two species of sabertoothed cat, timber wolves and extinct dire wolves, black bears, grizzly bears, and extinct short-faced bears. (Photo by Dale Toweill)

relative, the even-larger dire wolves. Grizzly and black bears were apparently common, as was the huge predatory short-faced cave bear. Ice Age North America was not a fun place to be if you were on the receiving end of attention by these species!

Bighorns coped with this myriad of soft-footed predators by developing keen eyesight and a reliance on "escape terrain"—habitats that included steep slopes covered in sharp and unstable rocks. Soft-footed predators like cats, wolves, and bears that chased prey couldn't effectively hunt the rocky cliffs, places where sheep could gain a safe rocky perch in a few jumps and stare nonchalantly down on a frustrated predator only yards distant.

By the time the last of the great glaciers retreated, bighorn sheep had become specialized to exploit the rich food that followed the retreating ice. Climates warmed first at lower elevations, forcing sheep to adapt ever more to mountain habitats even as the need to escape predators also forced them to specialize in exploiting rugged

To escape the wide variety of "soft-footed" predators (wild cats, wolves, and bears) that flourished during the Ice Age, bighorn sheep adapted to life among the sharp rocks and steep cliffs of the mountains. (Photo by Tim Bernard)

and rocky terrain. As the ice retreated for the last time and the fertile plains became progressively drier mammoths, muskoxen, camels, and even wild horses—and most of the predators—disappeared while modern bighorns, elk, bison, and pronghorns survived. Yet, as survivors of those ancient times, Rocky Mountain bighorns still carry the body shape and behaviors shaped by climates long changed and predators long extinct. The appearance and behavior of bighorn sheep today is as much a "fossil record" of those early times in North America as is any bone replaced by minerals.

Like bighorn sheep, elk moved from Asia into North America during the Ice Ages, feeding on the abundant grasses and leafy plants growing on rich soil exposed during periodic retreats of glaciers. (Photo courtesy Idaho Department of Fish and Game)

Only two species of bighorn sheep—Rocky Mountain and desert—are recognized by most scientists today. Audubon's bighorn, once believed to be a subspecies of Rocky Mountain bighorn sheep distributed along the badlands of the Great Plains,

The California bighorn sheep is a subspecies or "trophy type" of bighorn, adapted to arid Great Basin canyons and hills. California bighorns were easily accessible to early settlers, and were nearly exterminated by 1930. (Photo by Walt Van Dyke)

and California bighorns, animals of the isolated mountain ranges and river canyons of the Great Basin, are both now believed to be subpopulations of Rocky Mountain bighorns. Although Audubon's bighorn is now extinct, California bighorns are widespread and are managed as a unique "trophy type" of bighorn sheep by wildlife management agencies.

Audubon's bighorn, which occupied the breaks along the western edge of the Great Plains in North Dakota, South Dakota, and Nebraska until exterminated, was once considered a separate subspecies of Rocky Mountain bighorn. (Photo courtesy Boone and Crockett Club)

Chapter 3

The Life of Bighorns

Products of the Ice Age and shaped by a world full of dangerous predators, bighorn sheep have honed their senses and shaped their bodies to become masters of the steep and rocky environments they call home.

The sense of smell is far more developed in bighorns than in humans. Bighorns have a number of scent glands. The most prominent is the preorbital gland, a dark patch of skin just ahead of each eye, whose secretions appear to be highly individual. Bighorns also have scent gland between their toes, and rams have been seen, nose to the ground, following the trail of a reproductive ewe. Hunters tell of bighorns fleeing from wind-borne human scent at distances of nearly a mile.

Bighorns are alerted to danger by acute vision and smell. (Photo by Tim Bernard)

Hearing of bighorns is also acute. Bighorns live in a noisy environment—rocks fall and shatter, streams launch themselves over precipices in noisy clattering cascades, and winds scream incessantly as they hurl themselves against the mountains. Winds also whip sounds away from even closely associated sheep, so that bighorns rely little on sound for communication. Soft bleats function as contact calls between ewes and lambs and adults feeding together. Bighorns are attuned to unusual sounds, but usually rely on visual confirmation of the origin of such sounds before deciding whether to flee.

The eyes of bighorn sheep are large in proportion to the body and are prominent, giving the bighorn a wide range of vision. The dark spot just ahead of each eye is the opening of the preorbital gland, used in scent marking. (Photo by Tim Bernard)

Bighorns rely on vision to confirm the source of danger. (Photo courtesy Idaho Department of Fish and Game)

The vision of bighorn sheep is phenomenal. Keen eyesight is demanded of an animal that feeds in grasslands, and bighorns have very large eyes featuring a horizontal pupil that provides wide field of view. The eyes are especially attuned to detect movement, at distances that seem phenomenal to humans—an important consideration when life itself may depend on catching a flicker of movement from something intent on eating you.

With their highly developed sense of vision, bighorn sheep rely on eyesight for much of their communication with one another. Bighorns rely on a special signal to convey dominance, maturity, and physical condition. One key signal is horn size of rams. Horn size relates to power to physically dominate smaller rams and ewes, and it provides visual evidence of social status. Since horns grow throughout life, large horn size communicates accumulated knowledge and evidence of survival skills and since horn growth is related to nutrition and health, large horns indicate a physically powerful animal.

Bighorn sheep are very social animals. Social cues determine how sheep relate to one another, whether they are old friends or new acquaintances. Simply put, the largest-horned rams dominate all other sheep. Each ram lives in a social hierarchy where horn size indicates who gets first choice among grazing areas, favored bedding sites, and other privileges. When rams are of equal size, they

Rams spend the summer in areas providing high quality forage, which promotes growth of large horns. The largest-horned ram usually leads the group. (Photo by Tim Bernard)

may battle in tests of strength to determine their relative position, but small rams rarely dominate larger-horned rams. Because more mature rams nearly always have larger horns, they are expected to provide leadership. Young rams follow older, larger rams to learn about the best feeding areas, and they learn to negotiate their habitat using the most secure routes from the oldest survivors. An adaptation to living near the edge of retreating glaciers, where suitable habitat was fragmented and critical resources such as minerals were scattered throughout the unstable environment, this arrangement benefits the old rams too. Although young rams may compete for food, they are also vigilant in detecting potential predators.

Winter can be hard on bighorns, as they dig through accumulated snow to locate dried grasses and weeds. With little food available most bighorns slowly starve through the winter, relying on fat reserves stored during the summer and fall to survive until spring. (Photo by Dale Toweill)

Unlike rams, social structure among ewes is related to age. Ewes don't disperse among strangers, like the rams do. Female lambs typically remain with their mother in maternal groups throughout their lives, so every generation knows all other members of the group from birth. The oldest ewes know all the trails and feeding sites in the most secure and rocky terrain—areas where the survival of lambs is the greatest. Although all ewes are subordinate to even young rams with larger horns, ewes achieve social dominance based on maturity and body size. Younger ewes defer to older, and bigger, females.

Beginning in January when the rich grazing of summer and the excitement of the fall breeding season is past, the annual cycle of bighorn life is somewhat predictable.

Not all bighorns survive through the year. Some starve on winter range, others fall prey to predators, accidents or disease. However, the average mortality of adult bighorns is less than 10 percent annually. (Photo by Dale Toweill)

Winter is a time when bighorns focus on survival. Winter snows sap energy and cover most of the remaining food, forcing bighorns to dig deep to find the few cured stems that still retain nutrients. Winter is characterized by slow starvation, as bighorns eke out a minimal diet from cured grasses and shrubs. They spend long hours chewing and rechewing what little feed they find, as they try to minimize the loss of stored body fat, essential for survival.

Some bighorns don't survive winter. Mountain lions and coyotes kill some bighorns every year, and wolves, bears, and other predators all will kill bighorns given an opportunity. But predators usually avoid the steep rocky habitats bighorn sheep favor, since chasing surefooted sheep among the cliffs is rarely successful. Disease usually takes a far higher toll among bighorns, as animals weakened by disease consume their stored energy more quickly, and animals with low enregy reserves are most vulnerable to diseases. Even so, mortality among adult bighorns is usually low, ranging from 5 to 15 percent annually.

Bighorns eager for early spring forage will dig through the crust of early spring snows to find newly sprouting grasses. (Photo by Tim Bernard)

The warm days of early spring bring release from winter's starvation diet. As the soil warms, plants begin pushing new growth rich with nutrients above the ground. Bighorns eager for this rich source of food ignore the nutrient-depleted standing grasses and dig below the snow to locate and consume new plant growth.

The Life of Bighorns

By March, snow will have retreated from most winter ranges. Rams eager to exploit the rich flush of food on ridgelines exposed to the warming sun typically begin to leave winter ranges, and ewes, as they head toward higher country. Ewes, feeling the demands of new growth in their womb, begin to pay less attention to last year's lambs, which begin to travel more frequently with each other and older barren ewes than with their mothers. With high-nutrient food becoming more available daily, the youngsters become more active, engaging in play fights.

Ewes usually go off into rugged terrain alone to give birth to their lambs. (Photo courtesy Idaho Department of Fish and Game)

In May, heavily pregnant females separate from the group and isolate themselves in a secluded area among rocky cliffs one or two days before giving birth. Bighorn sheep have a long gestation period (175 days), which provides sufficient time for lambs to develop. Lambs are precocious, born fully formed and able to walk (and even run) within a few hours of birth.

Rams are the first to depart from winter range, seeking new food on the high, wind-exposed slopes where the soil warms early. (Photo by Dale Toweill)

The birth process itself is short, lasting only about forty-five minutes from the first appearance of placental membranes to expulsion of the lamb. Ewes lick the youngster to remove all traces of birth fluids and dry the coat. They may consume the placental membranes to restore lost nutrients and to remove a potential attractant for predatory animals. Twins occur only rarely.

Even young lambs are amazingly agile, able to run among the slopes and steep cliffs. (Photo by Tim Bernard)

Lambs weigh eight to ten pounds at birth and stand fifteen to seventeen inches at the shoulder. They grow rapidly on the ewe's rich milk. Ewes remain isolated with their lambs for a week or more, a time of maternal bonding when both become imprinted on the sound and scent of each other. After this bonding period, females with their new lambs rejoin the herd, forming a nursery group that will remain together into the summer.

Lambs grow quickly on their mother's nourishing milk. (Photo by Vic Coggins)

The Life of Bighorns

Growing lambs quickly gain strength and endurance, and by two weeks of age they can run with adults when danger is near. Danger for the lambs comes in many forms—accidents, predators (such as golden eagles, bobcats, and coyotes), and disease. Nearly half of each year's lambs are likely to die during the first year, and annual losses of lambs may exceed 80 percent during some years. Despite these high losses, usually enough lambs survive to replace annual losses among adults.

The rapidly growing lambs usually remain with their mothers during the first summer, but quickly become very alert, watching for danger. (Photo courtesy Idaho Department of Fish and Game)

Ewes delay shedding their winter coats until lambs begin to feed on their own, reducing the demands of lactation. The old winter hair falls off in clumps, pushed out by new hair growing beneath. Ewes look ragged and tattered during this process. Despite their tattered appearance, the process of shedding is a sign the ewe is replacing the nutrients lost through lactation earlier in the spring.

Summer is a time of relative ease for bighorn sheep. Lambs begin to eat plants early in the summer—although most will also nurse as long as the ewe will allow. Ewes feed long hours to restore nutrients needed to rebuild their skeletons and lay on fat for the coming winter. During this period, lactating ewes often form crèches (nursery groups), leaving their lambs in the care of older barren ewes. By entrusting the lambs to the care of "baby-sitters" they feed farther away from the security lambing cliffs, where feed is better. Once they've fed, the ewes return to watch over their lambs and ruminate.

Only when the demands of providing milk for the lambs begins to subside do the adult ewes begin to grow their summer coat, shedding the long hair of winter. (Photo by Tim Bernard)

Rumination is the process of rechewing tough grasses. As ruminants, grass-eating bighorn sheep have a complex four-part stomach. Bighorns swallow grasses and other leafy foods quickly while feeding. Only later do bighorns bring this material back to their mouths, rechewing the plant materials very carefully. This grinds the tough grasses into very fine particles, which are then swallowed and mixed with bacteria. Bacteria do what bighorn sheep cannot—they break down the plant fibers into simple molecules that bighorns can digest. This process requires hours of each day, hours the ewe typically spends with her lamb.

Young rams practice the skills they will need as adults. By the end of the second summer, when the little rams approach adult ewes in both body and horn size, they begin displaying dominance behavior to the two- and three-year-old females. Rams cannot mate without perfecting this dominance behavior, and they spend much time learning to spar and struggle among themselves and with older ewes, strengthening muscles and perfecting balance and footing. Older females tolerate little of this kind of nuisance, and quickly counter-attack and punish the upstarts.

All bighorns spend much of their time resting and rechewing their food, grinding it finer and finer so rumen bacteria can break down the plant fiber into products that can be digested. (Photo by Tim Bernard)

The Life of Bighorns

Young rams, such as the youngster at the lower right, follow older rams to learn where the most nutritious plants are found. (Photo by Dale Toweill)

When young rams are twenty-six to thirty months of age, most can dominate adult ewes. With their horn bases rapidly expanding, these young rams begin to stand out among the ewes. Ewes avoid the young rams, and soon they leave maternal bands, wandering into unexplored country. Most of the wandering young rams will encounter older rams and following them, learn new travel routes to rich feeding areas and the rules of ram society. Few young rams remain with the ewe and lamb groups after their third fall.

This period of initial separation is tough for young rams. Some wander for weeks without encountering older rams. In their loneliness, some will even be attracted to other species—horses, moose, even humans—only to be rebuffed; others may be attracted to domestic sheep, which often welcome the wanderers. Despite the actions of guard dogs and herders, which view the wandering rams as a nuisance or worse, the youngsters may join the domestic sheep band. Since the two species are closely related, they may interbreed. Bighorns may also contact livestock diseases or influenza from domestic sheep—and while domestic sheep have a high tolerance for influenza as a result of centuries of selective breeding, bighorn sheep often develop fatal pneumonia as a result.

> "With their horn bases rapidly expanding, these young rams begin to stand out among the ewes. Ewes avoid the young rams, and soon they leave maternal bands, wandering into unexplored country."

Young rams often wander during their second or third summers. They are often attracted to domestic sheep, and may even breed domestic ewes if opportunity allows. (Photo by Mark Fountain)

The onset of fall is heralded by frosts, which kill the growing grasses and leafy plants upon which bighorns feed. Food quality declines quickly, as plants reabsorb nutrients into the roots. The decline in food quality and the onset of winter weather combine to trigger bighorn movement toward lower elevations. Ewes typically arrive on the winter range in mid-to-late October while the rams, which often travel further, arrive several weeks later.

November brings on the breeding season, a time of intense activity and social behavior for bighorn sheep. It is a fascinating time to watch bighorn sheep, and a good opportunity to watch bighorn sheep communicate.

A young bighorn ram, freshly on his own after being expelled by adult ewes, approaches the author seeking companionship. (Photo by Dale Toweill)

The Life of Bighorns

Rams travel together on their seasonal migration from high elevation summer ranges to winter range, arriving in time for the November breeding season, or rut. (Photo by Tim Bernard)

Chapter 4
Communication and the Rut

Bighorn sheep communicate throughout the year, but much of the time their communication is subtle and unpredictable. During the rut, however, many displays are obvious. Rams spend nearly all their waking hours courting ewes and establishing or reasserting their dominance. During this period, most adult rams rarely even feed or ruminate, so intent are they on breeding.

To understand bighorn behavior it is necessary first to understand what is normal. Most of the time, bighorn sheep are relaxed around one another. Dominant animals may displace others from a favored feeding or resting area, but such actions are usually subtle, with few outward signals.

> "Alarmed bighorn often stand stiffly erect and may hop on all four feet, a behavior called "stotting."

The opposite extreme is alarm. Alarmed bighorn often stand stiffly erect and may hop on all four feet, a behavior called "stotting." Alarm behavior is clearly unusual, highly stylized and stereotyped. Such behavior attracts the attention of all other bighorns within sight, which stop other activities to watch. The alarmed bighorn typically gazes intently toward the noise or flicker of movement that caused its alarm, and other bighorns may follow its gaze. When any bighorn in the group finds reason to flee, the sudden activity usually panics the entire group. After brief initial scatter, most will follow the oldest ewe or largest-horned ram.

Bighorns typically orient themselves so that each animal is looking in a different direction to maximize the defense of the group. (Photo by Walt VanDyke)

Bighorns rely on steep escape cover for security. Most seem to calculate the distance between them and the threat on one hand, and escape terrain on the other. Bighorns may stand and watch a potential predator as long as it a safe distance away, but become terrified if it disappears from view. Although bighorns may mill about briefly while trying to relocate the threat, most will flee to avoid being stalked by a predator whose position is a mystery.

Bighorns typically follow the largest-horned ram in a group. He sets the pace; if others get slightly ahead, they wait for his leadership. He picks the daily feeding and resting areas as well. (Photo by Dale Toweill)

Unlike sight or sound, bighorns that scent a potential predator often flee at once. Scent is unmistakable, identifying an upwind threat.

In bighorn sheep society it is considered impolite—a threat—to stare. When bighorn sheep are relaxed and bedded, nearly every individual will lie facing a different direction. This behavior results in every sheep positioning itself so that the group has the maximum visual coverage of potential predator approaches.

It is considered impolite, even threatening, for any bighorn to stare at another. Even when bedded, bighorns typically orient themselves so that each animal is staring off into the distance—the better to detect possible threats to the security of the group. (Photo by Suzan Rogers)

Communication and the Rut

Bighorn communication sometimes relies on normal behaviors performed in a stylized manner. For example, a dominant animal of either sex may direct a stiff-legged foreleg kick at a subordinate. This weak kick is a sign of dominance, directed by a dominant animal toward a subordinate, and usually results in the subordinate animal quickly giving ground whether a feeding area or favored resting site.

Many dominance displays emphasize horn size. For example, the "horn present" is used by rams to assert dominance. The displaying ram stands stiffly erect and broadside to a subordinate, slowly tipping his horns from side to side. The displaying ram watches the subordinate carefully to ensure that the subordinate ram acknowledges the display with submissive behavior; if not, he will often follow up with other displays of dominance sometimes culminating in butting heads in a test of strength.

During the "horn present" a presenting ram holds his head high and slowly tilts his horns to emphasize their size. Note the posture of the ram in contrast with the ewes and young rams behind. (Photo courtesy Idaho Department of Fish and Game)

When rams first meet, most come together in a "huddle." Each ram displays his own horns while judging the size of the horns of other rams in the group. Huddles usually end amicably, as mature rams are keen judges of horn size and strength. Following a huddle smaller rams may rub their horns and foreheads against the horns and preorbital gland of the more dominant ram, transferring some of the dominant ram's scent onto their heads and confirming their status.

When rams come together, as individuals or groups, often the first behavior shown is the "huddle." In the huddle, rams all face toward the center of the group as individuals display their horns to one another. (Photo courtesy Idaho Department of Fish and Game)

Not all horn displays are equal. If neither ram signals subordinate status, one or the other escalate to a more serious threat. The "low stretch" is a serious threat, and often precludes a battle. It is also used by a very confident ram when wooing a ewe. In the low stretch, a ram pushes his chin forward while slowly tipping his horns from side to side so as to display their size. It's a display that emphasizes confidence and power.

Following the initial "huddle" and "horn present," smaller rams may rub their foreheads on larger rams, picking up scent from the larger animal's preorbital glands. (Photo by Tim Bernard)

Communication and the Rut

Of course, for displays of dominance to be effective, it is just as important for smaller rams to show submission. Submissive behavior allows smaller animals to stay within the group, enjoying the security the group provides when feeding and traveling, without having to risk injury as a result of battles. Submission is primarily a matter of communicating relative strength, and displays of submission allow younger bighorn time to grow within the security of ram society.

The "low stretch" is used by rams to assert dominance. Here a ram displays a low stretch to a ewe as part of the courtship ritual. (Photo courtesy Idaho Department of Fish and Game)

Displays that result in battles almost always occur between rams of approximately equal size—rams whose horns are so similar they don't know whether to signal dominance or submission. Since rams treat all smaller sheep like females, even displaying mock breeding behavior to confirm their status, the initial response is critical. Rams display repeatedly, reinforcing their status. A typical interaction might start with a horn display among equal-size rams. Even when the subordinate displays submissive behavior, the dominant animal may engage in a more assertive horn display (in the accompanying photographs, note how the dominant animal's head is held high while

Most displays occur between rams of about the same size. Here, one ram shows a "horn present" to another to which he has just delivered a foreleg kick, forcing the smaller ram to stand. (Photo by Dale Toweill)

The horn present is immediately followed by another head-up display. Note the smaller ram is looking away from the dominant animal, with his muzzle pointed downward. (Photo by Dale Toweill)

the submissive animal is looking down). The dominant animal may even mount the clearly submissive ram to further establish his position, thus signaling his relative position not only to his opponent but to all other group members as well.

Bighorn sheep are polygamous, with rams actively searching, identifying, and then defending, ewes in heat for the privilege of breeding during the November rut. Although rams typically arrive near the wintering area soon after the ewes and lambs, the sexes do not mingle freely—at least not initially. Mature rams typically spend their days near the winter range, but it is the young rams that first begin to mingle with the ewes.

When ewes come into estrous, hormones in their urine advertise their status. Rams can detect these chemicals via a special sensory organ (Jacobson's organ) embedded in their palate. A bundle of tissue and nerves connected directly to the bighorn's brain, the Jacobson's organ respond to female hormones, triggering male reproductive behavior.

As the breeding season approaches, young rams actively circulate among the adult ewes, performing dominance displays and often delivering a foreleg kick to a bedded ewe to get her to stand and urinate. Rams then taste the urine, and perform a "lip curl" to expose the urine to their Jacobson's organ. Ewes not in estrous are left alone while the rams circulate to other ewes. Ewes

Dominant rams treat all bighorns, ewes and younger rams alike, as females, even mounting younger rams in a breeding posture to reinforce their dominance. (Photo by Dale Toweill)

Communication and the Rut

soon tire of the constant harassment by young rams, and flee into the cliffs to avoid the youngsters. Often, the young rams follow.

While the youngsters are harassing the ewes, older rams reconfirm their dominance status. Rams of equal size attempt to outdo each other in dominance displays until both get so worked up that they "clash," or butt heads, to determine the stronger ram of the pair. Clashes are dramatic. Both rams square off, often rising on their rear legs before lunging headlong toward once another. Each ram uses his massive horns like a sledgehammer, striking the opposing ram on the outermost corner of his horns. The intent is to drive the smaller ram backward or lose its footing.

A dominant ram tests a ewe's urine to determine her reproductive status. The ram is showing a "lip curl." (Photo courtesy Idaho Department of Fish and Game)

The impact of horn on horn is like a gunshot, echoing among the hills for a mile or more. Both rams lift their rear legs as the horns come together, allowing the shock of the blow to dissipate through their bodies. These tests of strength may go on for hours, as the combatants grow increasingly weary. Misplaced blows open cuts that bleed freely. Only when one ram retreats—or darkness falls—do the combatants separate.

The "lip curl" enables the ram to determine the reproductive status of ewes. Urine of the ewe is tasted and the ram then curls his upper lip, exposing the highly sensitive Jacobson's organ in his palate, which responds to reproductive chemicals secreted by the ewe. (Photo by Tim Bernard)

As the breeding season approaches, harassment of ewes by the young rams and dominance displays among older rams coordinate the intensity of breeding activity. Ewes get into synchrony with one another, so that most enter

The "clash" is a test of strength between two evenly matched rams. The objective is to cause the weaker ram to stumble or fall. (Photo by Tim Bernard)

As clashing rams meet, each is balanced on his forelegs, allowing the energy of the blow to be dissipated through the body. Rams may clash repeatedly, hour after hour, until one animal withdraws. (Photo by Tim Bernard)

During the rut, rams will closely follow an estrous ewe until she is ready to mate. Other rams are often attracted by the commotion, joining the chase and even clashing to assert their relative dominance. (Photo by Tim Bernard)

Communication and the Rut

the peak of breeding at about the same time. At this point the larger rams join the ewes. When a ram finds a ewe approaching estrous, he immediately begins tending her, following her closely while showing dominance displays to discourage other rams from joining the couple. Often several rams will join in pursuit of the pair, and one or more of the rams may get distracted into a dominance battle while the ewe followed by another.

Clashes also commonly occur among rams during tending chases, when a ram is following or chasing a ewe. These "tending chases" attract an audience of rams, and one or more may challenge the tending ram. Usually it is a somewhat smaller ram that initiates such clashes after positioning himself uphill from the larger animal, using gravity to aid his blow. While two combatants are establishing their relative dominance, a third ram may enter the fray and either join the clashes or follow the ewe. At length the ewe stands for breeding. Despite the struggle and clashes that may attend the chase, in many cases it appear the she selects a ram from among her suitors. In fact, sometimes the ewe solicits the mating chase, stopping to rest periodically if the ram is exhausted.

> "The impact of horn on horn is like a gunshot, echoing among the hills for a mile or more."

Within a few days, ewes have conceived and lose their attractiveness to the rams. By then, many of the rams are exhausted from the frenetic pace of breeding. Some are seriously injured by misplaced blows. As fall merges into winter, demands for energy increase even as bighorns struggle to find enough food among the deepening snows of December.

Chapter 5: Bighorn Sheep Management

Bighorn sheep have been important to people since humans first occupied bighorn sheep ranges. Once incredibly abundant in some portions of their range, bighorn sheep were the basis for at least one entire culture of Mountain Shoshone Indians, the *tukadika* (Sheep-eaters) of the rough and forbidding northern Rocky Mountains. Bighorn provided the basis for this culture's entire economy, providing meat, skins for clothing and shelter, tools and implements made from bones and horn, and hundreds of individual products upon which these Indians relied, much as the bison did for other Indian cultures on the Great Plains.

With few laws to protect wildlife, tremendous numbers of animals were killed for meat, hides, horns, and sport prior to the twentieth century. (Photo courtesy of National Archives)

Petroglyphs featuring bighorns—rock art laboriously pecked into flat stone surfaces—are among the most common images across all western states, indicating the spiritual significance of bighorns to many cultures.

Bighorn sheep were very important to many of the American Indian tribes that occupied the Rocky Mountains. Pictoglyphs, such as these along Idaho's Snake River, often depict bighorn sheep. (Photo by Dale Toweill)

Miners needed fresh meat, and enterprising hunters could make a good living in much of the West by hunting. Bighorn venison was favored and brought premium prices from miners and settlers. (Photo courtesy Idaho Department of Fish and Game)

When western lands were opened to settlement in the nineteenth century, unregulated hunting of all big game animals—and especially bighorns—quickly took a toll on bighorn sheep populations. Meat hunters killed bighorns by the hundreds to supply mining boomtowns and settlements. Bighorn sheep venison was highly desired, and sold for premium prices. Hunting for trophies became a popular pastime near the end of the nineteenth century. Unregulated hunting soon took an additional toll on bighorns and other wildlife.

By 1880, huge bands of domestic sheep flooded Western rangelands. These animals fed on critical bighorn winter ranges summer and winter, destroying food upon which bighorn herds depended to survive severe western winters. Livestock also introduced diseases and parasites that drastically reduced or eliminated entire herds of bighorn sheep between 1870 and 1920. The repeated blows to bighorn sheep populations from unregulated hunting, loss of critical food, and disease was followed with a knockout punch as waves of human settlers converted critical winter range to ranches, farmlands, and communities that destroyed habitat and blocked traditional migration routes. Many diaries of the late nineteenth and early twentieth centuries comment on extensive losses of bighorns during severe winters.

Domestic livestock flooded Western states soon after the 1800s to supply mining towns and settlements with fresh meat. The newly introduced livestock consumed much of the food on winter ranges critical to bighorn sheep winter survival and spread disease and parasites to bighorns. (Photo courtesy of Idaho Department of Fish and Game)

By 1900 it seemed inevitable that bighorn sheep in the Rocky Mountains, like bison on the plains, were doomed. Had it not been for Theodore Roosevelt, it is unlikely bighorn sheep would have long survived the twentieth century.

Bighorn Sheep Management

Born into a wealthy family, Roosevelt dabbled in politics until personal tragedy early in his life resulted in his moving west, where he hunted and became owner of a cattle ranch before returning to political life. After returning to political office, Roosevelt was selected to run with William McKinley as vice president of the United States as a popular hero of the Spanish-American War. When McKinley was assassinated shortly after his election, Roosevelt became president.

Roosevelt's knowledge of the West and his passion for wild places and wild animals lead him to conclude that wildlife was a perpetually renewable resource if properly managed. Coining a new term, *conservation*, Roosevelt devoted much of his presidency to promoting conservation, or "wise management" of forests, rangelands, water and wildlife as a national and international agenda. As a result of his vision, national forests were set aside, national parks and wildlife refuges were established, and many programs were set in place to ensure that resources were managed as a *public trust*.

Roosevelt argued that government had an obligation to manage natural resources, forests, water and wildlife, just as a lawyer would manage the money in an estate. This obligation included protecting the principal of the estate (equated with natural resources) while managing those resources to provide an increase, the equivalent of monetary profits. The profits—the surplus produced annually—should be returned to the public, as owners, in the form of sustainable annual harvests—of trees, grass, and wildlife. This *public trust doctrine* comprises the basis for modern wildlife management.

Roosevelt set out to convince state governors that income from natural resources, such as timber for construction, grass for livestock, and wildlife for harvest, could break the "boom-and-bust" cycle all too prevalent on the western frontier. Users of the resource would pay a fee for access—and those fees would be used to manage the resources so they would produce sustainable crops of trees and grass and wildlife. It was an inspired concept, one that changed the future of the United States and the world.

Theodore Roosevelt, the twenty-sixth president of the United States and founder of the Boone and Crockett Club, made conservation of America's natural resources a national movement. (Photo courtesy of Boone and Crockett Club)

The underpinning to this concept was that the states, as trustees, would manage wildlife resources for the benefit of all citizens, and that funds for management would be drawn from the users of the resource (hunters) rather than from general taxes. This approach resulted in hunters paying for nearly all bighorn sheep restoration and management efforts.

By the 1920s nearly all Western states had laws in place to protect wildlife, and fledgling fish and wildlife management agencies. Most of the early effort focused on enforcing game laws to protect dwindling wildlife populations. (Photo courtesy Idaho Department of Fish and Game)

By 1920, nearly every state had an agency devoted to wildlife management, supported by the sale of hunting licenses and fees collected from violators. A national excise tax on sporting equipment was added in the 1930s, with the money directed to wildlife restoration. Fueled by dollars raised from hunters, the rebirth of wildlife populations across North America had begun.

Largely as a result of Roosevelt's insight, wildlife management agencies were created to restore dwindling wildlife populations as a continually renewable resource to be enjoyed by everyone. Restoration efforts were funded almost entirely by hunters. (Photo courtesy Idaho Department of Fish and Game)

Bighorn Sheep Management

Hunters, not taxes, have paid for nearly all bighorn sheep conservation and restoration efforts. Hunters pay for bighorn conservation directly through purchase of hunting licenses and tags and indirectly through an excise tax on sporting goods. (Photo courtesy Idaho Department of Fish and Game)

Hunting does not just play a part in wildlife management. Hunting is fundamental. Hunter's dollars paid for the restoration of bighorn sheep across North America, as well as other wildlife, whether hunted or not. Today, hunters raise millions of dollars annually to protect and improve wildlife habitat and to restore wildlife populations. Hunters play a critical role in protecting wildlife as a renewable resource for all to enjoy.

Restoration of bighorn sheep depends on protecting and managing habitat bighorns need. Bighorns need steep, rugged terrain, most of which has been little affected by humans. With habitat secure, the next priority is to restore bighorns to areas where they once lived.

Restoration always means capture of bighorns from healthy herds and transplant to areas previously occupied. Transplanting of bighorns began in the 1950s and accelerated after 1976, when fans of wild sheep created the Foundation for North American Wild Sheep specifically to raise money to aid wildlife agencies in bighorn sheep restoration efforts.

Wyoming's Whiskey Mountain was among the first sources of bighorn sheep for transplant elsewhere. Recognizing the value of this population, the state of Wyoming managed the bighorn population carefully to ensure that there were sufficient animals for transplant throughout Wyoming and other western states.

Bighorn sheep captured under this drop net on Whiskey Mountain near Dubois, Wyoming, were used as transplant stock for many of the initial transplants of bighorn sheep to areas where herds had been extirpated in Wyoming and other Rocky Mountain states. (Photo courtesy Idaho Department of Fish and Game)

But how do you safely capture wild sheep—especially when the goal is to capture many sheep at once? Many methods were attempted, but the first really successful methods was the *drop net*. Wildlife managers would erect a tall pole in a level area and then bait the area with a favored food item. Once the bighorns became accustomed to using the area the pole was used to support a huge net suspended like a circus tent over the feeding area. Ropes spreading the edges of the net were specially rigged to be severed simultaneously by blasting caps when bighorns were feeding below the net, which would then drop on the feeding animals. Confused and entangled in the net, the bighorns would be captured and restrained by biologists and loaded into trucks for transport to their new home.

Many states adopted dropnetting to capture bighorns from newly established and rapidly growing bighorn sheep herds, moving some of the animals to other vacant sites. (Photo courtesy Idaho Department of Fish and Game)

Bighorn Sheep Management

Although this method worked well, it was costly and time-consuming. A more portable method of capture was needed, and the *drive net* came in wide use. Wildlife managers propped long lines of portable nets on pole, creating a long funnel. Helicopters then chased bighorns toward the nets, gradually concentrating the running animals. As the sheep entered the wide mouth of the funnel, hidden capture teams entered behind them, pushing the bighorns into the nets, which fell onto the running animals, entangling them long enough for team members to capture and restrain each animal. Captured bighorns were then individually transported to waiting trucks. This technique was much more adaptable than drop nets, and could

Bighorn sheep, pushed by helicopters and by biologists on the ground, attempt to run through the drive nets, collapsing them and becoming entangled. Biologists quickly hobble and blindfold the animals to be transported to their new home. (Photo courtesy Idaho Department of Fish and Game)

Drive nets replaced drop nets as the preferred method of capturing bighorn sheep by the end of the twentieth century. Drive nets could be moved to areas that bighorn herds were using, and could be employed in much rougher terrain. (Photo by Dale Toweill)

The net gun allows specially trained biologists to fire a net over a single bighorn, entangling it and allowing it to be quickly captured and transported to a capture base where each animal is processed for transplant. Here biologists untangle a net after use. (Photo by Dale Toweill)

be quickly moved to wherever bighorns were concentrated. (Incidentally, drive nets were simply an adaptation of the sheep traps used centuries earlier by the Mountain Shoshone to capture bighorns for food.)

Today the favored method of capture is *net-gunning*. Using the speed and maneuverability of helicopters to locate bighorns, capture teams fire a specially designed net over each animal selected for capture. As the net falls and envelopes the running bighorn, the animal becomes entangled and a "mugger" (also riding in the helicopter) is let off nearby to restrain the animal. Within minutes, captured bighorns are transported by helicopter to a waiting crew of veterinarians and biologists speeding processing time and reducing the stress of capture. This technique maximizes opportunities for selective capture of only animals of the desired sex and age, and facilitates collection of biological data. Because the technique doesn't require a lot of costly field preparation time, capture efforts can be mobile and flexible, allowing teams to move from location to location in response to local weather and bighorn sheep movements.

After each captured bighorn is blindfolded and hobbled, it is loaded into a helicopter for transplant to the base of capture operations. (Photo by Dale Toweill)

Bighorn Sheep Management

Within minutes of their capture, Bighorns destined for transplant are individually examined by veterinarians. Each bighorn is individually examined for any injuries, blood and tissue samples are collected to determine health, and ewes are evaluated to determine pregnancy rates. Animals can also be inoculated against disease, and animals not desired for transplant can be immediately released. Best of all, the entire examination can be completed within minutes, reducing stress on bighorns and potential injury to the people involved.

Each captured bighorn is given a thorough checkup by a veterinarian before being released into the transport vehicle. (Photo by Dale Toweill)

Bighorn sheep await their release. Note the radio-collars on each bighorn. Biologists can follow the radio-signals emitted by the collars to individually locate each released bighorn. (Photo by Dale Toweill)

Bighorns selected for transplant are loaded in livestock trailers for moving to their new home. Often, several are equipped with a radio-collars that allow biologists to monitor their movements, verify areas used in summer and winter, and determine the number of lambs born the following spring.

The information (and more) is used to develop bighorn herd management plans. These documents identify management objectives including desired potential herd size and range.

Wildlife managers often address specific problems in bighorn habitats, as well. For example, bighorns eat grass, but over time some grassy areas are invaded by shrubs and trees that reduce the amount of food available and provide cover for predators

Released bighorns sprint for nearby rocky canyon walls. (Photo by Dale Toweill)

Bighorn Sheep Management

Controlled burns are used to improve bighorn sheep range, removing dead undigestible plant matter and making room for new plants to grow. (Photo by Vic Coggins)

to stalk bighorns. Periodic burning of these areas kills the invading shrubs and trees, and enhances the food supply while reducing the threat from predators.

In areas lacking sufficient water, water tanks can be installed to improve bighorn range. Mineral blocks can be added to supplement bighorn sheep diets, and can even be impregnated with medication to treat some diseases and parasites.

Wildlife managers have to deal with many other factors, as well. Bighorn sheep are wild animals, and their movements are not always predictable. They can be affected by drought and wildfire,

The completed "guzzler" high in Idaho back country features a water supply that will last through the summer months, allowing bighorns to summer far above domestic livestock. (Photo by Mike Foster)

Sometimes bighorn range can be improved by making water more readily available. Here, a team of workers fills rock around a drinking basin connected to a large reservoir high in bighorn habitat. The cover (background) will be fastened over the holding area to reduce evaporation. (Photo by Dale Toweill)

sometimes shifting their range unexpectedly. Dispersing young rams may simply wander away from established herds, seeking new habitats to colonize. However, while such movements are often beneficial, some may expose individual bighorns and even entire herds to risk.

For example, bighorns usually select habitats with nutrient-rich feed close to steep, rocky escape terrain. Unfortunately, that combination of factors sometimes attracts bighorns to highways where road banks provide rocky walls of escape terrain near ranches and farms. Highways may also be attractive because salt, applied to the road surface to melt winter snow, accumulates along highway ditches. In this type of setting, bighorns become vulnerable to vehicle collisions.

Bighorn Sheep Management

Even more dangerous, wandering bighorns may come into contact with domestic sheep or other livestock far from occupied bighorn sheep range. While many such contacts may have no adverse impacts, contact with domestic livestock poses some degree of risk of exposure to livestock diseases. Even contact with healthy domestic sheep may expose bighorns to bacteria, viruses, or parasites, some of which might result in disease among bighorns.

Wild, free-ranging bighorns are attracted to domestic sheep, but have few defenses against bacteria and viruses to which domestic animals are largely immune. This clipping dates from 1943. (Photo courtesy Wyoming Game and Fish Department)

Bighorn sheep select steep rocky slopes, and where these occur near a road, bighorn sheep may be struck by passing vehicles. (Photo by Dale Toweill)

Chapter 6: Where to Watch Bighorn Sheep

Bighorn sheep are sensitive to human intrusion. Even in areas with high numbers of bighorns, they can be difficult to locate and watch. However, bighorn sheep can become accustomed to humans. This process, called habituation, usually occurs over a period of years in areas where bighorns frequently encounter people and find them nonthreatening, as in a national park. Habituated bighorns often ignore humans entirely, allowing people to approach closely.

The National Bighorn Sheep Interpretive Center opened in 1993, a result of cooperation among the Wyoming Game and Fish Department, Town of Duboise, USDA Forest Service, Bureau of Land Management, and with the assistance of numerous conservation organizations and individuals. (Photo by June Sampson)

One of North America's premier locations for watching bighorn sheep is the Wind River Mountain Range in northwestern Wyoming. The seventy-five-hundred-acre Whiskey Basin Wildlife Management Area provides critical winter range for approximately one thousand bighorn sheep. From November through March bighorns occupy the open grassy slopes of eleven-thousand-foot Whiskey Mountain. The nearby National Bighorn Sheep Interpretive Center features informative exhibits about bighorn sheep and their management, plus educational materials for schools and guided tours of the bighorn range. The Center is operated by a nonprofit conservation organization dedicated to educating the public about the habitat and conservation needs of bighorn sheep. Staff of the Interpretive Association believe education is the vital first step in any effort to conserve bighorns. Additional information about the Center is available online at www.bighorn.org (or call 888-209-2795). The Center is located west of Dubois off Highway 26/287 within a short drive distance of Grand Teton and Yellowstone National Parks.

The Grand Slam of North American Wild Sheep is the first exhibit visitors see when they visit the National Bighorn Sheep Interpretive Center in Dubois, Wyoming. Exhibits and dioramas in the Center highlight biology and habitat requirements of bighorn sheep. (Photo by Dan Madden)

Where to Watch Bighorn Sheep

Many other national parks in the Rocky Mountains of the United States and Canada provide habitat for bighorn sheep. Perhaps the best opportunity to see bighorns is in Rocky Mountain National Park west of Denver, Colorado. Visitors often see bighorn sheep near Fall River west of Estes Park, and from Interstate Highway 70 near Georgetown. Bighorns are often visible from the highway in Yellowstone National Park on the slopes of Mount Washburn during summer months. Montana's Glacier National Park has good herds of bighorn sheep, often visible from the Going-to-the-Sun Highway. Bighorns also occur among the fantastic, eroded cliffs of Badlands National Park in South Dakota, and in South Dakota's Mount Rushmore National Memorial.

Outside of national parks, bighorns are commonly seen in Hells Canyon along the Snake River where it forms the border separating Idaho and Oregon. Visitors may take jet boat excursions into the canyon to see bighorns and other wildlife (tours begin in the Clarkston, Washington/Lewiston, Idaho area), and can visit the Jack O'Connor Museum at Lewiston's Hells Gate State Park to learn about bighorn sheep.

Canada's Rocky Mountain national parks (Jasper, Banff, Kootenay, Yoho, and Waterton) are home to about forty-five hundred to five thousand bighorn sheep. Visitors often have excellent opportunities to view and photograph mature rams. (Photo by Dale Toweill)

North of the border, Canada's national parks provide excellent opportunities to observe bighorn sheep. Jasper, Banff, Kootenay, Yoho, and Waterton National Parks are home to forty-five hundred to five thousand Rocky Mountain bighorns. Many herds in these parks are habituated to people.

Finally, many state and provincial wildlife management agencies maintain wildlife refuges and specially established public wildlife viewing sites. Many of these in the Rocky Mountains provide opportunities for visitors to see bighorn sheep. For details, contact the state wildlife management agency and ask for a copy of their wildlife viewing guide and other information on bighorn sheep.

Jet-boaters on the Snake River in Hells Canyon often see Rocky Mountain bighorns near the river's edge. (Photo by Dale Toweill)

Index

A
alarm 35
annuli 14
Asia 17

B
Banff National Park 61
Badlands National Park 61
bear, black 19, 26
bear, grizzly 19, 26
bear, short-faced cave 19
Bering land bridge 11, 17
Bering Sea 17
bighorn, Audubon's 20–21
bighorn, California 20–21
bighorn, desert 20
birth 27–28
bison 18, 20, 46
bobcat 18, 29
Boone and Crockett Club 12
Bow River, AB 11
breeding 35, 40, 43

C
camel 18, 20
capture 50–53
cat, saber-toothed 18–19
Cave, Natural Trap 18
  (see Natural Trap Cave)
cheetah, American 18–19
Clark, William 12
clash 41–42
conservation 47
coyote 18, 26, 29

D
Discovery, Corps of 12
disease 26, 29, 31, 46, 52, 57
dominance 25, 30–31, 35, 37, 39–41
drive net (see net) 51
drop net (see net) 50–51

E
eagle, golden 29
elk 20
escape 19
eyesight (see Vision) 12, 19, 24

F
Fall River, CO 61
foreleg kick 37, 39–40
Foundation for North
  American Wild Sheep 49

G
gestation 27
Glacier National Park 61
gland, scent 23
goat, mountain 18
goats 18
Going-to-the-Sun Highway 61
Grand Teton National Park 59
Grey, Robert 11

H
habituation 59
hearing 23
height 12, 14
Hells Canyon 61
highway 56
Himalaya Mountains 17
hooves 15
horn display 37–40
horn present 37
horn size 12–13, 24
horns 12–14
horse 18, 20–21
huddle 38
hunting 42, 48–49

I
Indians, Mountain Shoshone 45, 52
Indians, Sheep-eater 45

J
Jacobson's organ 35, 40–41
Jasper National Park 61
Jefferson, Thomas 11–12, 17

K
keratin (see Horns) 13-14
kick, foreleg (see foreleg kick) .. 37, 39–40
Kootenay National Park 61

L
lamb 13, 28–29
Lewis, Meriwether 12
lion, American 18–19
lion, mountain 18–19, 26
lip curl 35, 40
livestock 31–32, 46, 57
low stretch 38–39
lynx 18

M
Mackenzie, Alexander 11
mammoth 12, 18, 20
management plan 54
mating chase 42–43
McGillivray, Duncan 11
McKinley, William 47
mineral block 55
Mississippi River 11
Mount Rushmore National Park 61
muskoxen 18, 20

N
National Bighorn Sheep
  Interpretive Center 9, 59
Natural Trap Cave, WY 18
net, drive 51
net, drop 50–51
net-gun 52

O
organ, Jacobson's 35, 40–41
  (see Jacobson's organ)
Ovis canadensis 11

Index

P
parasite 46–47
Peace River, BC 11
petroglyph 45
pneumonia 32
pronghorn 18, 20
public trust 47

Q
Quaternery Period 12

R
restoration 49
Rocky Mountain National Park 61
Roosevelt, Theodore 46–47
ruminate 30
rumination 30
rut 33, 35, 40

S
scent (*see* Smell) 12, 23, 36, 38
Shaw, George 11–12
sheep, domestic 31–32, 46, 57
sloth, ground 12
smell 23
Snake River 61
starvation 26
stotting 35
submission 37, 39–40

T
tank, water 55
tending 43
tiger, Siberian 18
Tukadika 45

V
vision 12, 19, 24

W
Waterton National Park 61
weight 12, 14
Whiskey Basin Wildlife
   Management Area, WY 64
Whiskey Mountain, WY 64
wolf, dire 19
wolf, timber 18–19, 26

Y
Yellowstone National Park 61
Yoho National Park 61

Suggested Reading

Clark, James L. 1964. *The Great Arc of the Wild Sheep*. Norman: University of Oklahoma Press. 247 pp.

Geist, Valerius. 1971. *Mountain Sheep: A Study in Behavior and Evolution*. Chicago: The University of Chicago Press. 383 pp.

Geist, Valerius. 1975. *Mountain Sheep and Man in the Northern Wilds*. Ithaca, N.Y.: Cornell University Press. 248 pp.

Geist, Valerius, and Michael H. Frances. 1993. *Wild Sheep Country*. Minocqua, Wisc.: NorthWord Press, Inc. 176 pp.

Gildart, Robert C. 1999. *Bighorn Sheep: Mountain Monarchs*. Minnetonka, Minn.: NorthWord Press. 143 pp.

Mitchell, Richard M., and Michael R. Frisina. 2007. *From the Himalayas to the Rockies: Retracing the Great Arc of Wild Sheep*. Huntington Beach, Calif.: Safari Press, Inc. 223 pp.

Toweill, Dale E., and Valerius Geist. 1999. *Return of Royalty: Wild Sheep of North America*. Missoula, Mont.: Boone and Crockett Club and Foundation for North American Wild Sheep. 214 pp.

Valdez, Raul. 1982. *Wild Sheep of the World*. Mesila, N.Mex.: Wild Sheep and Goat International. 186 pp.

Valdez, Raul, and Paul R. Krausman, eds. 1999. *Mountain Sheep of North America*. Tucson: The University of Arizona Press. 353 pp.

Author's Biography

Dale E. Toweill is a professional wildlife biologist with an abiding passion for wild sheep and their management, and has authored and edited both *Return of Royalty: Wild Sheep of North America* (published by the Boone and Crockett Club in 1999, and winner of the 2005 CIC Literary Prize) and *Desert Bighorn Sheep* (published by Nature Trails Press in 2003). Other books include *North American Elk: Ecology and Management* (Smithsonian Press, 2003), winner of awards from the Wildlife Society and the American Library Society, and *Perspectives on Biodiversity* (published by the National Academy of Sciences in 1999). In addition, he has authored dozens of book chapters and hundreds of articles on wildlife topics. Dr. Toweill received his doctorate in wildlife ecology and management from Oregon State University, and currently lives in Idaho where he continues his involvement with wild sheep.